Small Studio • Great Impact

SOLO • 2UO • 3RIO

Edited & published by
Viction:ary

W0009681

viction:ary

When asked by viction:ary to write a foreword for this soto-2uo-3rio book I thought the best contribution would be to describe how my own studio operates.

Firstly the biggest challenge for me in running a successful design studio is to remain small in size. This way one stays (relatively) independent and keeps a maximum capability of the door open to freedom.

Neubau is defined by a systematic approach to type and designing for systems. The studio operates through commissions alongside self-initiated projects, developing design and typography for print, screen and space.

To people, Neubau is mainly known by its worldwide published archive and resource books. The fact that these books became bestsellers managed to trigger global attention generating a growing group of followers and new customers.

Over the last decade of Neubau operating in Berlin I have had the privilege to work for a large group of international clients — a wide range of projects, big and small — and to collaborate with some of the most skilled and best designers with a variety of cultural backgrounds. My collaborators come from all corners of the world including Norway, Sweden, Japan, the Netherlands, Switzerland, Portugal, Ireland, Spain, France, Austria, Germany, the United Kingdom and the United States.

Having started as a solo design studio in late 2001 a total of 35 collaborators adding to the Neubau family until now is quite a surprising figure to me. It would actually make an average of three new assistants per year, while in fact the standard setup is me with one assistant or business partner. But depending on the nature of a project, Neubau can expand to a group of 20 specialists.

Even if the actual team in Berlin is kept as small as possible it is great to know that Neubau established a vivid network of Neubau associates around the globe. While the growing group of collaborators is mainly caused by our extensive Neubau Archive book series, smaller units usually execute the commissioned work. In order to keep Neubau's daily business alive and in full swing it was necessary to have additional people involved for realising the Neubau books. Since 2003 my co-workers helped me with such voluminous books like *Neubau Welt* (2005), *Neubau Modul* (2007) and *Neubauism* (2008).

Apart from the original past projects that unified us here in Berlin, we are all curious people that share the love for archives, systematic approaches, books, the smell of freshly printed ink on paper and typography. The fact that no one does books like Neubau, people working here are united by a sort of confidence that we belong to a very special, small but extremely privileged "club".

Although the list of contributors is extensive I still find the most satisfying and pleasant team size to work within is three people. In a small unit everyone keeps the big picture in sight and gains overview of the overall process and knows what is going on. This way everyone learns the most from the others involved and creates a productive working environment.

STUDIO SPACE

Neubau is located in a typical factory building, sharing a generous studio space of 200 square metres in the heart of Kreuzberg, Berlin. This will possibly only last as long as the monthly rent remains reasonable in a city being more and more gentrified and dominated by impertinent real estate speculators.

NEUBAU DESK SETUP

Our studio desks I designed in a way that they are easily modified in size and usually organised in what we call "project-islands". This way the team sits in a circle almost like around a (digital) fireplace (being our computers). Everyone sees the other members involved while working behind the screen. Decisions are made easily without having too many meetings in our conference room. By keeping the operative part as low and dynamic as possible helps me remaining a designer instead of just ending up in endless meetings as a studio manager.

BLOCKED STUDIO PHONE NUMBER, NO CELLULAR PHONE NOR TWITTER OR FACEBOOK ACCOUNT

In 2013 we still don't have the luxury of "a secretary" to answer the studio phone which is why the Neubau telephone number remains secret to the general public. Initially new commissioners get in touch via email first therefore.

Also up to this day I don't own a cellular phone, which I am very happy for. Luckily enough my clients don't have problems with that since they know that they can reach me anytime via email or studio phone.

There are usually five to ten projects in the making at one time. Dealing with customers from different continents and time zones works very positive for us since they are usually behind our local time — with Asia being the exception. Apart from staying up late the time differences enables Neubau to work for physically closely and more distant located clients simultaneously.

Finally, the fact of having an impact as a small studio without getting naked for the camera, or being on the latest blogs or social networks is quite simply that big things come in small packages.

. . . .

Stefan Gandl, Neubau (NeubauBerlin.com)
Berlin, Germany

Set up as Stefan Gandl's own studio in 2001, Neubau adds Christoph Gruenberger in 2006. Their first solo exhibition "Neubauism" was opened by legendary designer, Wim Crouwel, at MU, The Netherlands, in 2008.

AKATRE
Paris, France

Key members / Valentin Abad, Julien Dhivert, Sébastien Riveron
Specialties / Graphic design, Typography
URL / www.akatre.com

Est. 2007

"To be competitive is to be different and to follow your way."

Akatre is the creative playground of French trio, Valentin Abad, Julien Dhivert and Sébastien Riveron, who claims almost a traditional approach in their graphic responses through hand-drawings for type design or hand-built installations for a physical touch in their 2D images. Taking pleasure in re-examining matters, every project makes for Akatre's lab for creative expressions in graphic, typography, photography and web design, for themselves and clients in fashion and cultural fields.

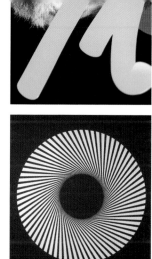

10ᵉ FESTIVAL DES CINÉMAS DIFFÉRENTS
DE PARIS - DU 9 AU 14 DÉCEMBRE 2008

-TU
NAN
TES

9 MARS
AVRIL 2012

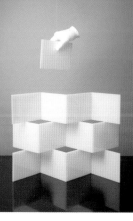

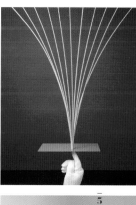

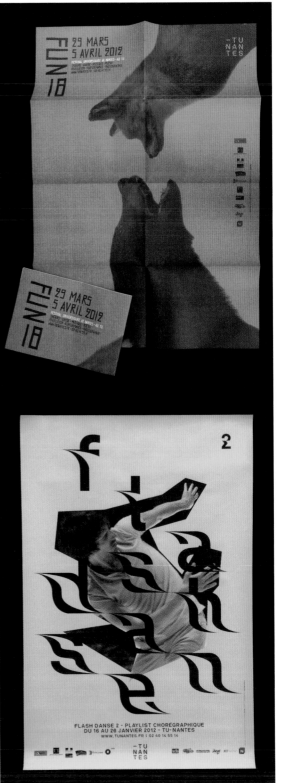

HOW DID YOU START YOUR COMPANY? WHAT IS/ARE YOUR CREED(S) AND ASPIRATION(S)?

We met when we studied art, which was where project "Akatre" started. After our graduation in 2006 and a year of internship and working as creative assistants we decided to work together. It was very important for us to create with our own tools in all of our projects, including types and image-making.

We do graphic design, typefaces, photography and film. Akatre in French makes an echo to the paper format (A4) and it also means that we are four — the three of us in the studio and our client's involvement in the process.

WHAT HAS BEEN DIFFICULT FOR YOU AT THE BEGINNING?

At the start it was hard to impose our way of working on the clients because when you are a young designer, clients usually take you as an executant so this is the hardest time when you have to impose yourself and convince the client that your idea or graphic solution is a good one for the project. But that's the way it is, clients will never come to you because you have never done what he would like... In a way it's normal but it's sad.

01

WHAT ROLES DO YOU INDIVIDUALLY PLAY IN THE FIRM?

About administrative tasks, each of us tries to have an equal share. With the clients, the three of us go to every briefing and it is the same with the press. When a project is validated, one of us will lead the project to the end and deal with the client.

HOW DO YOU PROMOTE YOURSELF?

Good question, we don't really promote ourselves as a big company would. We do it the old way through word of mouth. And also we participate in all the publications we are offered to participate. Our website and all the participative blogs are also important for our visibility.

02

TU-Nantes - Scène de recherche et de création contemporaine
Théâtre et danse - www.tunantes.fr - 02 40 14 55 14

03

WHAT MAKE(S) SMALL STUDIOS
SUSTAINABLE? WHAT IS MOST CRITICAL
FOR STUDIOS LIKE YOURS TO GAIN A
FOOTHOLD IN THE COMPETITIVE
MARKET?

Small studios are certainly sustainable because
of their creativity and their potentiality to dare.
To be competitive is to be different and follow
your way.

We think that big agencies can be creative but
sometimes clients are afraid and don't want to
take the bet. For big projects there are a lot of
people involved so it's really hard for a good idea
or a good graphic design to eventually come to
light. But sometimes when the creative team
stands, it totally works. We would love to work on
this kind of project.

IT MIGHT BE EASIER FOR LARGE DESIGN
AGENCIES TO WIN A JOB. WHAT ARE
YOUR STRATEGIES TO BEAT THEM? HAVE
YOU EVER LOST HAD TO GIVE UP AN
OPPORTUNITY THAT MIGHT BE
RELEVANT TO YOUR COMPANY SIZE?

Our strategy is to keep our way of thinking, and
try to be as creative as possible. The marketing
arena doesn't have to take the power against
the creativity. We are really not dealing with the
same clients or on the same job so there is no
competition.

WHAT ARE THE BEST AND WORST
EXPERIENCES BY FAR?

Our best experience is probably our artist-in-
residency experience in the south of France
near Marseille, where we had the opportunity to
work on a personal project. We spent four days
in different spots doing a photographic project,
Sphère 2012. We carried a big mirror sphere,
measuring 2.5m in diameter, in desertic spots.
Our bad experience does not come from a par-
ticular incident but the moments when a project
slides from our hands. But it doesn't happen
often (we try to!)

ARE YOU THREE VERY DIFFERENT
INDIVIDUALS?

Yes, we are different because we draw inspiration from different worlds and different fields
but that's what make our creative process interesting. But then we're attracted by the same
aestheticism.

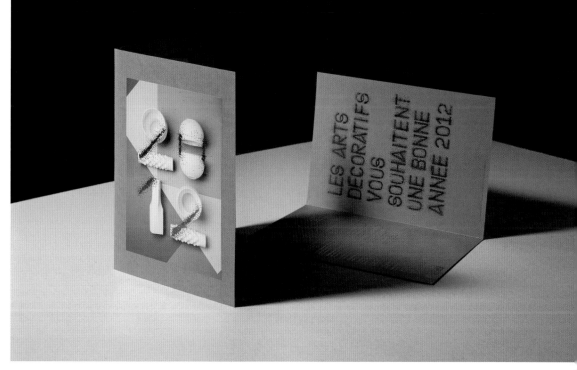

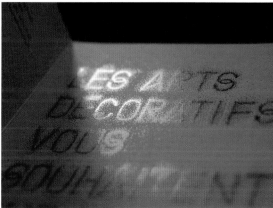

We went to the same school so we had the same training. We elaborate every project together. When a project is validated, one of us take the project to the end, always with the other two at the downstream.

If we are standing at three extremes and fail to reach a consensus, we will discuss and try to convince one another or find a new direction together and start again from zero.

DO YOU INTEND TO RETAIN YOUR PRACTICE'S CURRENT SIZE? IF IT HAS TO GROW BIG ONE DAY WHAT WOULD BE THE ULTIMATE SIZE?

We don't need to expand our company for the moment but we can't say never because we don't know what's going to happen in the future.

We love to create and have our hands in the dirt if you know what we mean. The heads of a bigger company would only be telling others to work things out in your way and stop doing things themselves. We are scared of that...

AND THE TRADITION(S) ETHOS TO KEEP?

Ideas, rigour and fun. Rigour and fun seem to be opposite but we really think it's the basis of our work.

05

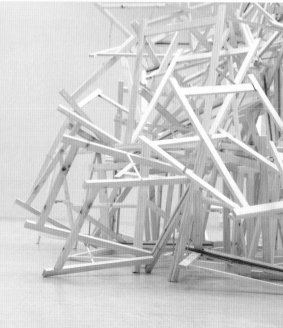

06

07

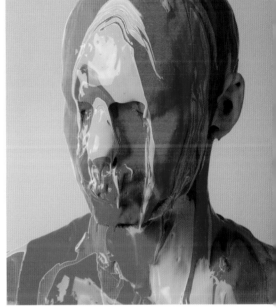

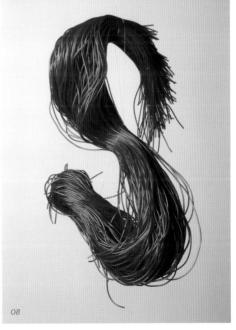

08

ANYMADE STUDIO
Prague, Czech Republic

. . . .

Key members / Petr Cabalka, Filip Nerad, Jan Šrámek aka VJ Kolouch
Specialties / Graphic design, Photography
URL / www.anymadestudio.com

. . . .

Est. 2008

Founded in 2008 in the Czech Republic, Anymade Studio is comprised of Petr Cabalka, Filip Nerad and Jan Šrámek aka VJ Kolouch, who "ANYtime MADE work full of smile and fun". Each distinct with a knack for different fields of visual arts, together they synthesise all their creative efforts into an eclectic collage of illustrations, graphics, cut-outs, videos, motions and sounds of odd texture for clients in music and fashion industries.

"The best is having complete trust from a client while you can do what you want."

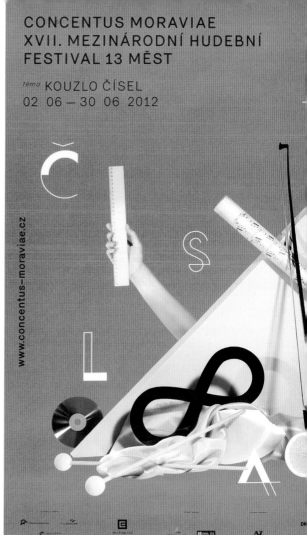

CONCENTUS MORAVIAE
XVII. MEZINÁRODNÍ HUDEBNÍ
FESTIVAL 13 MĚST

téma KOUZLO ČÍSEL
02 06 — 30 06 2012

www.concentus-moraviae.cz

XVI. MEZINÁRODNÍ
HUDEBNÍ FESTIVAL
13 MĚST

téma ČESKÉ SNY
OTISKY A VZPOMÍNKY
28 05 — 25 06 2011

CONCENTUS
MORAVIAE

moraviae.cz

www.concentus-moraviae.cz

01

HOW DID YOU START YOUR COMPANY? WHAT IS ARE YOUR CREED(S) AND ASPIRATION(S)?

That's a nice question. Anymade was born out of a strong belief and desire which still last. Before starting our own firm, sometimes we got a job from an agency, but mostly it was terrible — nothing really creative and fun. So we said that we would rather do nothing than go on like that. We started Anymade right after we finished our studies.

WHAT HAS BEEN DIFFICULT FOR YOU AT THE BEGINNING?

It was very difficult to get interesting and well-paid jobs and that's still a challenge.

WHAT ROLES DO YOU INDIVIDUALLY PLAY IN THE FIRM?

Our roles are equal. We share everything so that each of us can focus on his strong points with respect and support from one another.

HOW DO YOU PROMOTE YOURSELF?

We do almost nothing. We have a web page and a Facebook page where we post our current work but the rest goes its way. Our largest promotional activities are perhaps having our own exhibitions and partaking collective exhibitions, festivals, parties etc.

WHAT MAKE(S) SMALL STUDIOS SUSTAINABLE? WHAT IS MOST CRITICAL FOR STUDIOS LIKE YOURS TO GAIN A FOOTHOLD IN THE COMPETITIVE MARKET?

We are trying to do our job well and we believe this energy will bring the right contracts in return. I think that the biggest advantage of small studios is their distinctively individual style and that's how we gain a foothold in the market.

02

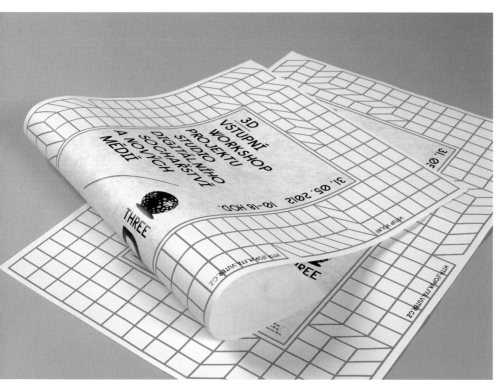

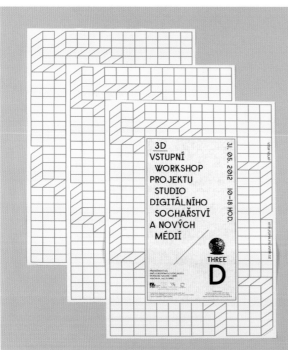

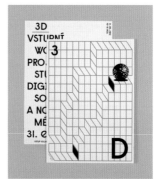

04

03

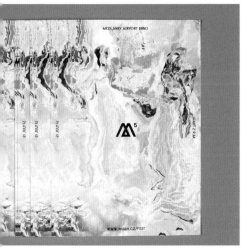

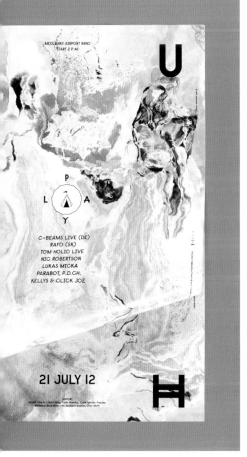

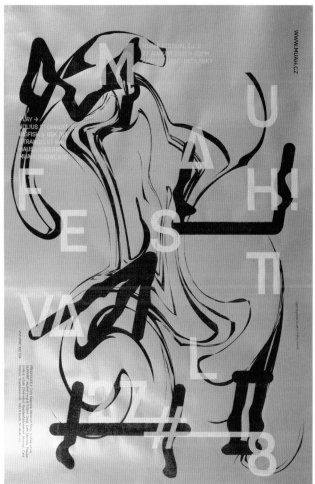

05

IT MIGHT BE EASIER FOR LARGE DESIGN
AGENCIES TO WIN A JOB. WHAT ARE
YOUR STRATEGIES TO BEAT THEM? HAVE
YOU EVER LOST HAD TO GIVE UP AN
OPPORTUNITY THAT MIGHT BE
RELEVANT TO YOUR COMPANY SIZE?

Large design companies work on different
ground and in many ways it's impossible for us to
compete with them. We usually get contract on
the ground of reference when people approach
us with a specific idea and they want it to be
made by us. Rarely we take part in bidding wars.
Recently we are trying to avoid it because condi-
tions like having a lot of studios in a competition, no sketch money, a big amount of work,
unqualified jury etc. in our "geographic region"
aren't very friendly. Sometimes we take part in
exclusive competitions with maximally three
other studios where only experts will decide
whose idea works the best.

WHAT ARE THE BEST AND WORST
EXPERIENCE BY FAR?

The best is to have complete trust from a client
while you can do what you want. Then the process can go really easy. The worst is the opposite.
Disaster :).

ARE YOU THREE VERY DIFFERENT
INDIVIDUALS?

Definitely. We all do something a little bit different. We influence each other. That's what pushes
us forward and we enjoy it.

HOW DO YOU THREE WORK TOGETHER?
WHAT WOULD YOU DO IF YOU ARE
STANDING AT THREE EXTREMES AND FAIL
TO REACH A CONSENSUS?

We have known each other for a long time and
we cooperate really well. I don't even remember
a moment when we couldn't reach a consensus.
Simply, it works.

DO YOU INTEND TO RETAIN YOUR
PRACTICE'S CURRENT SIZE? IF IT HAS TO
GROW BIG ONE DAY, WHAT WOULD BE THE
ULTIMATE SIZE?

We will see. We're already cooperating with
others and we enjoy it every time. It's inspiring
for us. For a long time we have searched for
someone who could take care of our production.
Do you know anyone? :)

AND THE TRADITION(S) ETHOS TO KEEP?

Quality and playfulness. To work in one studio
with your best friends.

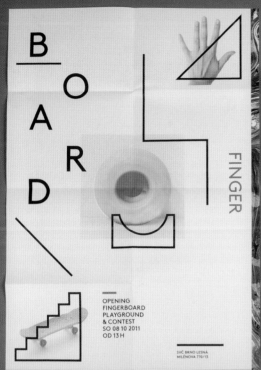

„Darovali jsme objekt
všem těm, kteří mají rádi
fingerboarding. Koncipovali
jsme ho nejen jako urbanistický
plán nekonkrétního města,
ale také jako fingerboardový
skatepark. Je to hřiště, nad
kterým má možnost potkávat
se určitá subkultura. Objekt je
odteď možné vidět v zahradě
Centra Volého Času, na
Milénově 13, brněnské části
Lesná (Čertova rokle, konečná
tram. č.11)"

Anna Balážová

„Darovali jsme objekt
všem těm, kteří mají rádi
fingerboarding. Koncipovali
jsme ho nejen jako urbanistický
plán nekonkrétního města,
ale také jako fingerboardový
skatepark. Je to hřiště, nad
kterým má možnost potkávat
se určitá subkultura. Objekt je
odteď možné vidět v zahradě
Centra Volého Času, na
Milénově 13, brněnské části
Lesná (Čertova rokle, konečná
tram. č.11)"

Anna Balážová

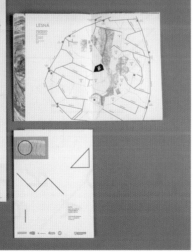

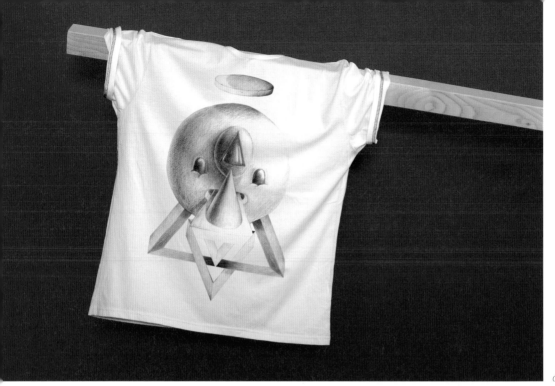

07

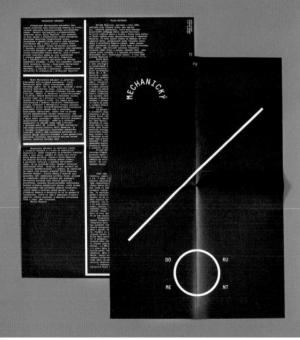

08

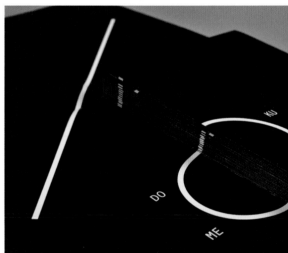

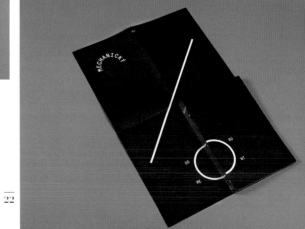

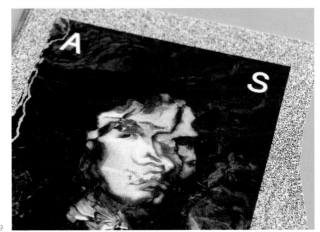

09

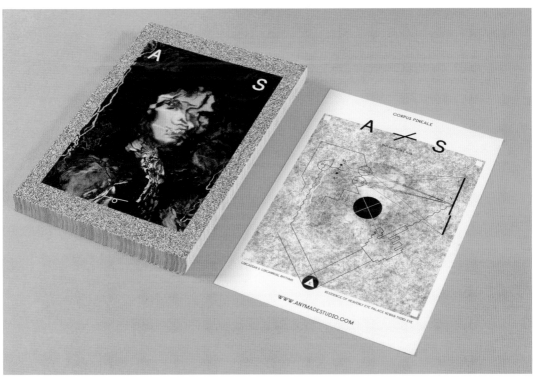

"We want to create work that we're proud of... that pushes our clients to do something extraordinary."

ARTWORKLOVE
Paris, France

Key members / Caroline de Vries, Ben Reece, Marion Laurens
Specialties / Art direction, Graphic design
URL / www.artworklove.com

Est. 2009

Artworklove is English and French art directors and designers, Ben Reece, Marion Laurens and Caroline de Vries, who approach design based on artistic experimentation and systematic design structure with emphases on craftsmanship and a balance between functions and forms. Over the years the studio has conceived visual identity, prints and digital materials for clients, including The Barbican Sound and Music, Champagne Krug and Princesse Tam.Tam.

HOW DID YOU START YOUR COMPANY? WHAT IS/ARE YOUR CREED(S) AND ASPIRATION(S)?

We've known each other for many years and worked on common projects for Neville Brody's Research Studios in Paris and London. So we already knew we would be a good fit together. When the time came to start our own studio it felt very natural for us to work together and we understood each other creatively. It felt right to work in Paris as many of our favourite projects and clients were sited there. We started with a small office above a dance studio and grew from there.

We want to create work that we're proud of, that is smart and well crafted, that pushes our clients to do something extraordinary and they're ultimately really happy with. We want to have great experiences and hopefully make some great connections with the people we work with. We're interested to see where our work can take us both intellectually and physically and we think that part of life is being able to do something different every day (well, most days anyway).

WHAT HAS BEEN DIFFICULT FOR YOU AT THE BEGINNING?

We started the company in a very organic way, with a gradual shift from freelance work. We had almost no overheads to begin with as we had our own equipments and were given office space at a production company that we worked for. One of our first problems was realising the limits of what we could achieve as a small company. We would dedicate all our time to pitches that were exciting but beyond the scope of our resources. Sometimes this would work out but other times we would lose weeks of productive time on projects. Realising that we needed partners for bigger jobs was also an important step. It was challenging to figure out how we could work as three art directors with equal responsibilities. We chose a democratic model which worked out most of the time.

01

02

03

04

WHAT ROLES DO YOU INDIVIDUALLY PLAY IN THE FIRM?

We are all art directors, graphic designers and account managers. We have a very intimate setup so everyone has to look after all aspects of the work and the running of the studio. Based on our experience there are some jobs that are more naturally suited to one or another of us, but most of the time we just learn from each other and share everything.

HOW DO YOU PROMOTE YOURSELF?

We don't do a lot of self-promotion. Sometimes blogs pick up our work and we're comfortable with that, but most of our commissions come by word of mouth. We tend to be quite humble so we haven't really submitted any work to competitions or magazines. Books invite us to submit work but we think that it's mostly other graphic designers who see this. That's OK with us. We've often thought of getting someone who could look after new business for us, but it's a very sensitive role and we have never found somebody who is exactly the right fit.

WHAT MAKE(S) SMALL STUDIOS SUSTAINABLE? WHAT IS MOST CRITICAL FOR STUDIOS LIKE YOURS TO GAIN A FOOTHOLD IN THE COMPETITIVE MARKET?

Small overheads are a very good idea. We never had debt in the studio and this let us do things we want most of the time. In terms of competition, it's something we've only been aware of in creative pitches. I think small studios should probably steer clear of pitches whenever possible, it can be a very demoralising way of getting started. Small studios have to rely on word of mouth so it's important to make sure that clients are happy at the end of a project. It's also useful to be able to use resources from bigger firms on large projects, we've partnered with advertising companies and in-house creative departments on many jobs, which let us get on with what we're good at.

06   07

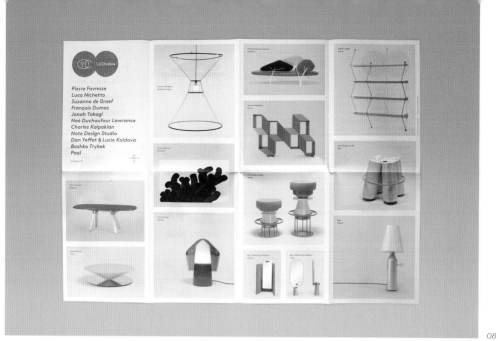

08

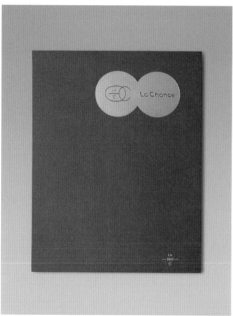

IT MIGHT BE EASIER FOR LARGE DESIGN AGENCIES TO WIN A JOB. WHAT ARE YOUR STRATEGIES TO BEAT THEM?

We present ourselves as a small boutique agency with tailored design solutions. In meetings it's usually very clear if we're passionate about a project and I think that, for the most part, clients want something unique and crafted with care that has traces of a dedicated creative agency. I think clients are usually won over by the idea that their project is very important to us, as we don't take on hundreds of projects. Apart from this we're not very bureaucratic. We don't charge for sending out PDF files or adding a small deliverable to the project scope. We're always available and we're very intimately involved in all our projects. I suppose a client who already has the experience of working with a small agency would probably find it easier to hire us. Sometimes big businesses need to communicate with other big businesses and we don't try to get in the way of that.

HAVE YOU EVER LOST HAD TO GIVE UP AN OPPORTUNITY THAT MIGHT BE RELEVANT TO YOUR COMPANY SIZE?

Yes, we've always tried to make a bigger team when necessary but for some clients, size matters. Many times they get started on jobs with bigger corporate agencies and then come back to us when they realise that's not what they want.

09

WHAT ARE THE BEST AND WORST EXPERIENCES BY FAR?

The best experience is always working on a project where the content really excites us and we're making work that challenges us. This happens most of the time, so our best experience also occurs when we feel really proud of what we do.

Every agency has probably dealt with the same bad situations — projects which go on way longer than anticipated due to internal problems with the client; clients who don't pay because they have cash flow issues or they've changed their mind on a design solution that has been signed off and developed; fake pitches where the client just wants to see some ideas with no intention of taking the work any further... All these things happen pretty rarely but they still happen and they're much more painful for a small studio. Smaller design agencies should obviously try not to put all their eggs in one basket, either financially or creatively. This is a big risk.

TRIPTYCH:
THE MUSIC OF
ELIANE RADIGUE

12—26 JUNE 2011
LONDON

Sound and Music

10

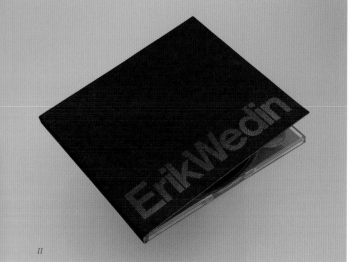

11

ARE YOU THREE VERY DIFFERENT INDIVIDUALS?

Marion and Caro are French and Ben is British. this is already a very different starting point in terms of attitude, experience and education. Caro comes from a photographic background and Ben worked for some time on moving-image projects. Marion has worked more on packaging projects, and tends to be more illustrative in approach — but these are differences in application and process. In terms of taste and solutions, even if we do start out from different places we tend to meet in the middle, so there're lots of overlap in the things we appreciate and the ways we like to work. Of course we are all really different people but part of the reason we work together is that we like spending time with each other. This helps us enormously to come to creative agreements. Our conversations and different points of view, although sometimes heated or conflicting, are a part of the developmental work on every project.

HOW DO YOU THREE WORK TOGETHER? WHAT WOULD YOU DO IF YOU ARE STANDING AT THREE EXTREMES AND FAIL TO REACH A CONSENSUS?

If somebody feels especially strongly about something they may peel off and work on something separately with some of the studio resources, but almost always we find a way to mix and adapt our individual approaches. This happens naturally through conversation or application. All of us feel fairly comfortable with our output and so there's no wars of ego, etc..

DO YOU INTEND TO RETAIN YOUR PRACTICE'S CURRENT SIZE? IF IT HAS TO GROW BIG ONE DAY, WHAT WOULD BE THE ULTIMATE SIZE AND THE TRADITION(S) ETHOS TO KEEP?

I'm not sure we'd like to grow much bigger, but if we did I think it would have to be something that happened naturally. We'd like to keep a very human approach and the sensitivity to detail that we've had so far.

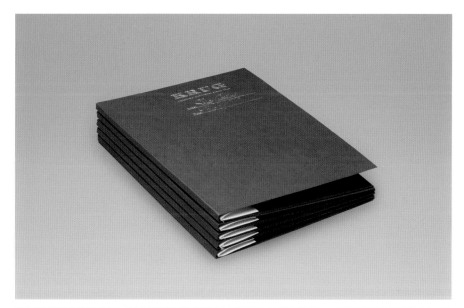

01, 03 / Kenzo Parfums_2009
Kenzo concept store identity and packaging created at Research Studios Paris.

02 / Princesse Tam.Tam_2011
Press dossier for Princesse Tam.Tam flagship store opening in Paris.

04 / MyQueen_2009
Alexander McQueen perfume packaging developed at Research Studios Paris.

05 / Nouveaux Regards sur le Sud_2012
Identity and typographic system for a photographic expo. Exhibition concept by PomPomPom (now renamed PAM).

06 / Alpen Glow Music Summit_2011
Collateral for a music event with Austrian and UK experimental performers.

07 / Virna Cirignano Identity_2011
A modulable, scalable system for a dance and theatre event producer.

08 / La Chance Visual Identity_2012
Complete identity system and catalogue 2012 for a furniture company.

09 / 101 Things to do This Summer_2011
Identity and publicity materials for Barbican Centre's summer programme.

10 / The Music of Eliane Radigue_2011
Collateral for Eliane Radigue's first retrospective by Sound and Music.

11 / Erik Wedin Identity_2010
Logo and collateral for Swedish composer and musician.

12 / Krug Press Dossier_2011
Collation of Dutch artist Scarlett Hooft Graafland's work for 'Krug Lovers' campaign.

"In many ways
we are a well-kept
secret — and
probably more in
Denmark
than abroad."

DESIGNBOLAGET
Copenhagen, Denmark

....

👤👤👤 🏴

Key members / Claus Due, Christina Holm,
Lukas Muellner
Specialties / Art direction, Graphic design
URL / www.designbolaget.dk

....

Est. 2002

Designbolaget is a Danish design
studio working at the intersections of art,
fashion and culture. Founded
by Claus Due in 2002 and now extended
to include project manager Christina Holm
and graphic designer Lukas Muellner, the
Copenhagen-based team has built a truly
colourful portfolio accented by publication
and identity design with carefully
executed details and tactile finishing.
Conceptual thinking and constant dialogues
with clients lay the strong ground for
their original designs.

HOW DID YOU START YOUR COMPANY? WHAT IS/ARE YOUR CREED(S) AND ASPIRATION(S)?

Designbolaget was established exactly ten years ago (by 2012 fall). I (Claus Due, founder of Designbolaget) was working at some advertising agencies but did not really feel like I belonged there. I had this dream on how wonderful my life would be if I could only work with things that interested me — and that was art, music and the visual universe around the fashion industry.

I made a small calculation: cutting down my expenses and working from my home designing album sleeves and occasionally an art catalogue for the local art museum and I would be the happiest boy in the world. The small setup in the beginning made it possible for me to say no to projects that did not 100% match with my interests and work only for clients that I could really identify with. And then I guess it just went on from there. When you put all your energy into a few fields of design, you will suddenly end up being part of something — developing a relationship with people you like to work with, whom will also recommend you to somebody else and so on. With a lot of my clients I have been working for 6–7 years and I love, it means a lot to me.

WHAT HAS BEEN DIFFICULT FOR YOU AT THE BEGINNING?

The difficult thing about running a design studio is definitely to stick to your ideals. Make everyday a good day, be inspired — meet inspiring people AND whether you like it or not, deal with the business side of things. You have to make money to support your family and now employees.

01

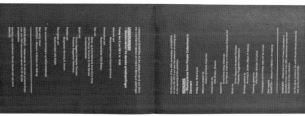

WHAT ROLES DO YOU INDIVIDUALLY PLAY IN THE FIRM?

I, Claus Due, am the founder, creative director, art director and graphic designer. As for now I am lucky to have two very talented and experienced guys working with me. Christina is our project manager and Lukas is a graphic designer. Lukas solely works on graphic design, while Christina plans budgets and our time: who should be doing what and when. She keeps in touch with all the magazines and blogs and finally is a really good business developer for me. Keeps a helicopter view on things when I am being too emotional about some things.

HOW DO YOU PROMOTE YOURSELF?

The recognised London-based design blog *It's Nice That* reviewed Designbolaget recently, stating "Designbolaget is Denmark's best kept design secret, and it's wonderful". And they are right. In many ways we are a well-kept secret and probably more in Denmark than abroad. Until now, we have been promoting ourselves only by participating in and winning international design awards. But we want to change this now. With Christina on board since January 2012 we now have time and resources to promote Designbolaget in diverse ways. This year (2012), we relaunched our website, promoted the site in all the cool international design blogs, built up a Facebook profile and joined the Danish Design Association. We just started writing news and articles about our clients and we are very excited about all these actions since this is indeed a new step forward for us.

02

03

04

05

WHAT MAKE(S) SMALL STUDIOS SUSTAINABLE? WHAT IS MOST CRITICAL FOR STUDIOS LIKE YOURS TO GAIN A FOOTHOLD IN THE COMPETITIVE MARKET?

The capacity of keeping costs low while the work's quality high is one of the main advantages being a small studio. Also, we believe that the service level and relationships with clients in general are much more personalised. The border between "clients" and "friends" is not that distinct at Designbolaget as it would be in larger companies. It can be a challenge from time to time, but our feeling in general is that we have the nicest clients in the world!

The critical part in being a small studio is of course the span in qualifications. It's impossible for us to be two steps ahead in all kinds of disciplines within the design field. We have then very specifically, defined our primary skills — art direction and graphic design at the intersection of art, fashion and culture with a focus mostly on printed matter.

IT MIGHT BE EASIER FOR LARGE DESIGN AGENCIES TO WIN A JOB. WHAT ARE YOUR STRATEGIES TO BEAT THEM? HAVE YOU EVER LOST HAD TO GIVE UP AN OPPORTUNITY THAT MIGHT BE RELEVANT TO YOUR COMPANY SIZE?

Our strategy is to specialise in the fields of art, fashion and culture, and constantly keep the quality of our work as high as it can get. We really believe that, in order to survive in the competitive market, we have to strive for an extraordinary level of quality in every piece of work we do, on a daily basis — this is the advantage of being a small studio. We are able to take a much more uncompromising approach to our work than many of the large agencies. Recently, we gave up a newbizz project competing among others including a great, big design agency. The deadline was all too tight and would have been impossible for us to handle while still running our daily business with other clients. We really had a hard time giving it up and at the same time we felt very relieved. In this specific case the bigger agency is of course better off.

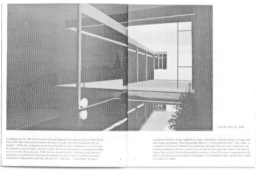

06

07

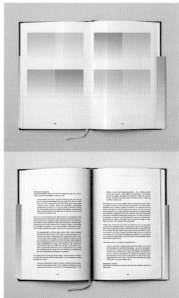

08

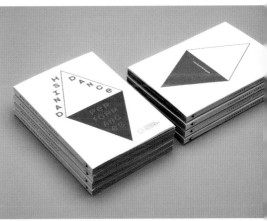

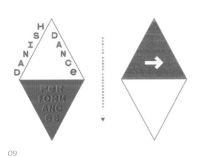

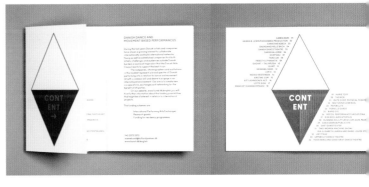

WHAT ARE THE BEST AND WORST EXPERIENCES BY FAR?

Best experience is, when a process has been good — when you really hit it off with a client, a photographer or a colleague. The worst is, when money issues take over your life and you have to struggle with the economy at times — even let people go. It takes away your energy, ruins the flow and creativity.

ARE YOU THREE VERY DIFFERENT INDIVIDUALS?

YES indeed!

Claus Due is definitely the energy booster bringing all kinds of ideas and thoughts on music, design, art and culture into the studio. Being the founder and creative director, Claus is undoubtedly the most important personality when it comes to clients. Project manager Christina is trying to catch her best ideas regarding the studio and implementing them in terms of the overall ongoing decisions concerning strategy and communication. Together with graphic designer and Austrian native Lukas, he is representing a more structured and detailed approach to projects. Lukas would probably deny it, but he brought some Swissness to the studio, even though he is from some place else.

HOW DO YOU THREE WORK TOGETHER? WHAT WOULD YOU DO IF YOU ARE STANDING AT THREE EXTREMES AND FAIL TO REACH A CONSENSUS?

In general we work very well together. But since Claus is the owner of the place, he, of course, has the final say. But the idea of standing at three extremes seems quite unrealistic. At least two of us would agree on any given topic!

DO YOU INTEND TO RETAIN YOUR PRACTICE'S CURRENT SIZE? IF IT HAS TO GROW BIG ONE DAY, WHAT WOULD BE THE ULTIMATE SIZE AND THE TRADITION(S) ETHOS TO KEEP?

The ultimate size for Designbolaget is a maximum of four people plus interns. It is a difficult size being this small. We want to do killer projects every time — work in the field of culture or fashion AND on top of that, earn some money to pay the rent and salaries. You tend to work a lot.

Designbolaget never gets big or otherwise it wouldn't be the Designbolaget as we know and love. So many complex layers are put on top of a business when it gets bigger. The focus on design wouldn't be the same. And that is what we are here for — creating stunning design.

10

11

12

42

01 / Skagens Museum Identity_2007-
Exhibition catalogues, stationery, etc. for Skagens Museum and its centennial.

02 / KUNSTEN Museum of Modern Art_2009-
Quarterlies, signage and catalogues for the museum and its 40th birthday.

03 / BZR_2010
Visual concept and campaign for BZR, a sub-label of Bruuns Bazaar. Photos by Sacha Maric.

04, 07 / Won Hundred_2012-
Art direction and collateral for a Danish fashion brand. Photos by Sacha Maric.

05 / Søren Lose: Relicts_2011
Catalogue for Søren Lose's new work exhibition at Kunsthallen Brandts.

06 / The Future Begins at Home_2011
Catalogue for Danish artist Asmund Havsteen-Mikkelsen's exhibition.

08 / Just Noise._2012
Exhibition design, catalogue, etc. for Mads Gamdrup's exhibition.

09 / Danish Arts Council_2012
Materials promoting Danish performing arts at International Tanzmesse 2012.

10 / Seeing is Believing._2012
Catalogue for Søren Dahlgaard's exhibition at Kunsthal Brænderigården.

11 / Baum und Pferdgarten_2012
Lookbook for fashion brand Baum und Pferdgarten's 2012/13 collections.

12 / Moshi Moshi Mind_2009-
Visual Identity and packaging for a lifestyle sub-brand of Moshi Moshi.

13 / Gallerie Møllerwitt Identity_2004-
Stationery, website, invites and exhibition identity for Gallerie Møllerwitt.

13

"Our aspirations are to feel good about what we do, and that our work has purpose and makes people smile."

IWANT
London, UK

Key members / John Gilsenan,
Louise Moe-Dean, Dawn Gardner
Specialties / Branding, Art direction
URL / iwantdesign.com

Est. 2003

IWANT is an award-winning multidisciplinary creative design agency based in East London. Specialising in branding, art direction, model making, set design, illustration and graphics. IWANT speaks ideas in an original complex of colours, imagery and typefaces. John Gilsenan, the studio's founder, has freelanced in Prague for two years before setting up IWANT in 2003.

Having studied fine art I stumbled into graphic design through flyer and record sleeve design. I managed to get an entry-level job at an agency when after a year I had the opportunity to go and live abroad, where I began to freelance. I started the company when I returned to the UK. Freelancing was a great experience but I didn't feel the long hours of working alone were good for me creatively. I am more sociable than that and interaction with others helps with all aspects of creative process.

The company was initially run from my basement in Stoke Newington, London before we found another space. It was all a bit of naive fun — we had no plan, no idea and I didn't have a great deal of design skill. I really was learning and blagging as I was going along. I also didn't really have much background knowledge of designers, design agencies or anyone to ask for advice — it was all very green.

If we had a creed it would be to work hard and enjoy what you do, remain relevant and strive to continue learning and improving always. Our aspirations are to feel good about what we do everyday and to feel that our work has purpose and makes people smile.

WHAT HAS BEEN DIFFICULT FOR YOU AT THE BEGINNING?

Early difficulties were very much down to the above and to have experience working in only one studio (before starting my own practice), for a short period of time. I now know I would have been better equipped early on if I had worked in a couple more different studio environments to gain better insight into running a business and gather more knowledge, experience and skills it would have made the transition into running my own studio smoother without doubt.

WHAT ROLES DO YOU INDIVIDUALLY PLAY IN THE FIRM?

The members of our current team are creative director, John Gilsenan and designers, Louise Moe-Dean and Dawn Gardner.

John is the creative director who runs the business, designs, illustrates, drinks coffee, oversees and approves all creative work. Normally each of us manages on-going regular client work, and comes together on larger projects to ensure we all have input and freedom to express our ideas. As in any small studio we are all wearing many hats the entire time — you have to, to make it work.

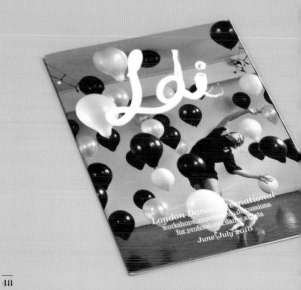

HOW DO YOU PROMOTE YOURSELF?

We have never really promoted ourselves other than through credits on the work we do. We have only recently started sending out e-news, and designed and built a website that is actually fit for the purpose after existing with a succession of holding pages. We haven't really needed to worry about promoting our name. I guess we're a little lucky but we also try to really look after the clients that believe in us. The work we do is generally very visible in the public — events, festivals, records, which get seen and breed interest. I'm in no way suggesting that zero promotion is a good thing, not at all. Promotional work is a great way to be creative without client restrictions and boundaries and show a broader audience, including potential and existing clients, what you can achieve.

WHAT MAKE(S) SMALL STUDIOS SUSTAINABLE? WHAT IS MOST CRITICAL FOR STUDIOS LIKE YOURS TO GAIN A FOOTHOLD IN THE COMPETITIVE MARKET?

Small studios are sustainable for many reasons. Low overheads mean you don't have to become slaves to work. You can be more careful about the projects you take on rather than snatching at every possibility to ensure you have enough money coming in to pay lots of salaries. This then affords you flexibility with clients and their budgets and develops a more intimate relationships with clients — you can get to know them and work closely with them. I feel a lot of small agencies that grow too quickly often lose a little of the edginess that made them interesting to begin with.

I think it is critical that new studios have a clear goal at the outset. This comes from the experience of not having one — even if this shifts later on — and they should understand their motivations and aspirations. In a partnership scenario a clear outline of one another's goals, aspirations and work ethics is imperative to avoid unhappy marriages — I think there is a stat that 70% of partnerships fail and generally it is down to differences in attitudes to work and individual goals; also, a strong sense of identity — where you see your studio's position within the industry — is also important to help you attract the type of clients you want to work with. There's no point in setting up a practice and getting lots of the 'wrong' kind of work.

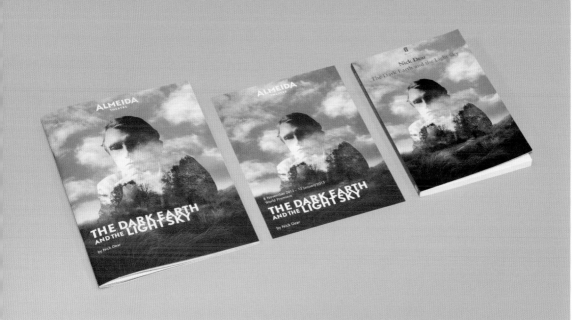

8.8.12
ONE YEAR ON

OUT OF THE ASHES
A
SELECTION OF FREERANGE
RARITIES & DELETIONS
Cat Number : FRBOXSET01
Barcode : 823670040011

I'm not sure we ever know whom we are pitching against in advance — does anyone? This is probably a good thing as I would rather focus on what we do well rather than worrying who we are competing with.

Without over-stressing we are a small agency we do play on our size and the differences a smaller agency can offer — no account handlers, only direct access to your designer. You won't have a big fancy pitch by the creative director and then get palmed off to an intern or junior. Sometimes people get it, sometimes they don't. Your folio is also a great weapon (we have worked with a premiership football club, large art institutions and global brands), which shows immediately and clearly that we can manage projects of scale.

I do know we have lost pitches because of our size and have been told so by the client. I know we have lost pitches to Peter Saville, Neville Brody and some of our peers we really respect, but it can be good to know you are in the frame with some of these people to begin with. It boosts you for the next opportunity. We have also retrospectively received jobs from some clients, who initially worried about our size but eventually liked our pitch because we gave a good account of ourselves. On a couple of occasions where we initially lost to a really big gun and then got taken on to run aspects of the projects or take over the project part way through.

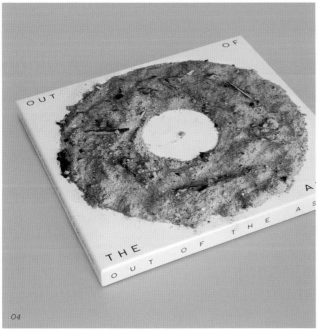

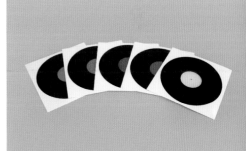

04

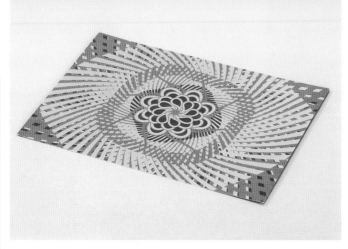

07

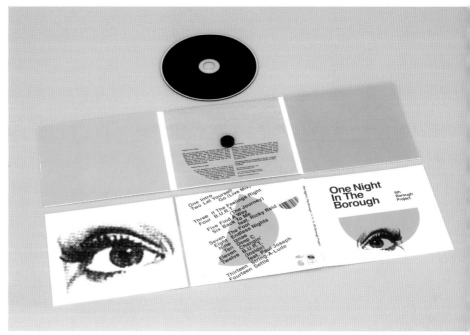

08

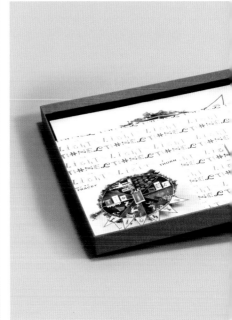

WHAT ARE THE BEST AND WORST EXPERIENCES BY FAR?

The best and worst times are closely related. The company was initially a partnership, and although it worked well early on, for various reasons it became increasingly difficult to manage relationships and over several years the partnership broke down as many do. The worst time was accepting and dealing with this whilst managing a company, remaining professional and looking after clients' needs. The best time was getting through to the other side of this, taking sole control of the company and pretty much starting again with a new vision and outlook.

ARE YOU THREE VERY DIFFERENT INDIVIDUALS?

Yes, we are all quite different. Louise and Dawn have more in common as they are of a similar age. I don't think they appreciate my musical obsessions (or tastes) but they will put on a brave face. We have different tastes in most things but we all get on and we complement one another. The common thread is we all grew up in Essex.

HOW DO YOU THREE WORK TOGETHER? WHAT WOULD YOU DO IF YOU ARE STANDING AT THREE EXTREMES AND FAIL TO REACH A CONSENSUS?

We work individually on some projects and with some clients, and come together for larger, more creative new work. We discuss the projects and then go our separate ways to develop thoughts and concepts before putting it all together to discuss some more. Everybody has a say in everything but ultimately if we are at a stalemate, I will make the decision and explain why — it of course can then still be up for discussion if feelings are strong.

DO YOU INTEND TO RETAIN YOUR PRACTICE'S CURRENT SIZE? IF IT HAS TO GROW BIG ONE DAY, WHAT WOULD BE THE ULTIMATE SIZE?

I don't intend to make IWANT a massive agency, but we will get a little bigger. We will have four permanent staff from January 2013 — with a dedicated administrator joining in to free up my time a little more, and over the next year we may look into taking on another designer, but I think once you get to a certain size the chances are you begin to snowball. We'll take it as it comes naturally rather than forcing the issue.

AND THE TRADITION(S) ETHOS TO KEEP?

Don't become slave to work, don't stop experimenting and if you stop enjoying it, give up and do something else.

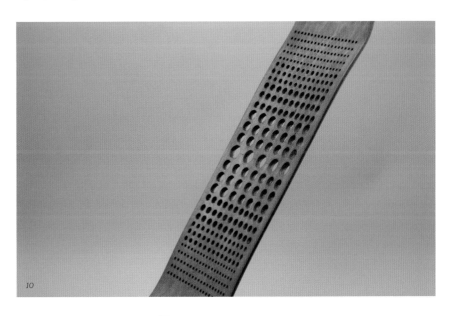

10

11

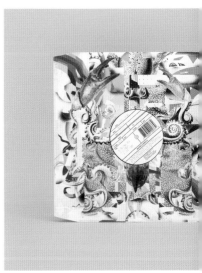

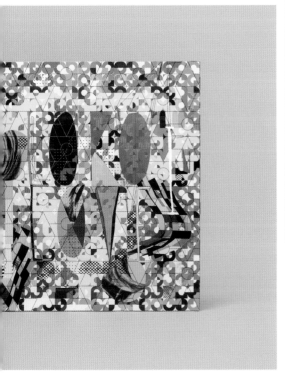

12

01 / Secret Codes and Battleships_2012
Bespoke type and illustrations for Darren
Hayes' album campaign.

02 / London Dance International_2011
Third and final instalment of London
Dance International.

03 / Almeida Collateral_2012
Art direction and publicity materials for
Almeida Theatre.

04 / Out of the Ashes_2012
Packaging for a special box set referenc-
ing a devastating blow at Sony Music's
Enfield warehouse.

05 / Session Victim_2012
CD and triple pack vinyl for Scottish electronic house artists Session Victim.

06 / SAM First Season Brochure_2009
Installation and brochure design for
Sound and Music.

07 / Film London Invitation_2010
Invitation for Film London's launch party
in Mumbai.

08 / Delusions of Grandeur_2012
Album design for electronic house artists,
6th Borough Project.

09 / Tinsel and Lights_2012
Tracey Thorn's X'mas album campaign
with a shadow box and bespoke types.

10 / Cherryvale Skateboard_2010
Custom design for Cherryvale's collabora-
tive project.

11 / Buzzin Fly_2010-12
Assorted design for Buzzin' Fly Records.

12 / SERIOUS_2012
Season branding, merchandise, etc. for
BBC Radio 3 London Jazz Festival 2012.

13 / A Coming of Age_2010
Sophomore album for British pop band,
Lucky Soul.

13

LE CREATIVE SWEATSHOP
Paris, France

· ·

Key members / Julien Morin,
Mathieu Missiaen, Stéphane Perrier
Specialties / Scenography, Visual identity
URL / lecreativesweatshop.com

· ·

Est. 2009

"Create new media, and make ourselves indispensable."

Le Creative Sweatshop is a Paris-based creative studio committed to
originality and quality at the crossroads of fashion, design, contemporary art
and architecture. Having its world developed around fixed and dynamic
works of volume, the team has most of their pieces hand-produced which gives
them a humble, precious and fragile stature. The group of three also enjoys
interacting with a network of partners specialising in photography,
retouching and clay modelling, etc..

HOW DID YOU START YOUR COMPANY? WHAT IS/ARE YOUR CREED(S) AND ASPIRATION(S)?

Our company started three years ago with Mathieu and Julien after a meeting for personal jobs, until the Nissan advertising job, done in hands with famous French photographer, Grégoire Alexandre. Since then, we worked on several projects with a lot of new clients (Hermès, Cartier, Orange, Nissan…) and started a still life photo blog (http://cinqfruits.tumblr.com) which allows us to do new editorials.

With all these projects, Le Creative Sweatshop was ready to accept all kinds of work — be it window displays, data information design or experiments with new materials and rendering. In future, we would want to launch all kinds of stuffs, like an interactive magazine or new blogs and media in order to expand our activities and originality.

WHAT HAS BEEN DIFFICULT FOR YOU AT THE BEGINNING?

At the beginning, it was not easy to be able to start big projects, and average techniques weren't part of the equation. Since then, with hard work and new skills, all things seem easier to work out.

WHAT ROLES DO YOU INDIVIDUALLY PLAY IN THE FIRM?

Mathieu is our art director and photographer for our daily blog, where Julien gives art directions too, and takes care of everything technical. And I, Stéphane, am assistant art director and graphic designer. We all work together since two years ago, and we hope it'll last.

HOW DO YOU PROMOTE YOURSELF?

Our usual promoting routine: Facebook, Twitter, Tumblr, Instagram.

01

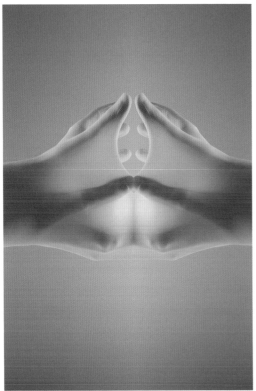

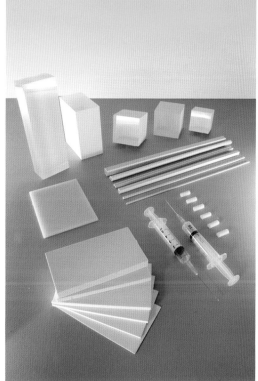

WHAT MAKE(S) SMALL STUDIOS SUSTAINABLE? WHAT IS MOST CRITICAL FOR STUDIOS LIKE YOURS TO GAIN A FOOTHOLD IN THE COMPETITIVE MARKET?

We think originality, a lot of experimentations and availability are the keys to be part of the equation with bigger firms. We create new media, make ourselves indispensable.

IT MIGHT BE EASIER FOR LARGE DESIGN AGENCIES TO WIN A JOB. WHAT ARE YOUR STRATEGIES TO BEAT THEM? HAVE YOU EVER LOST HAD TO GIVE UP AN OPPORTUNITY THAT MIGHT BE RELEVANT TO YOUR COMPANY SIZE?

There is none. We've been in the industry for three years and our work speaks for itself. We don't want to struggle with big firms because big firms and small studios take two different jobs.

We lost two or three big projects but it was not about our motivation — it's because we were young. Whether or not there was a lack of confidence towards small studios was not relevant. Big projects don't lead us to grow our studio but we have to work more efficiently.

03

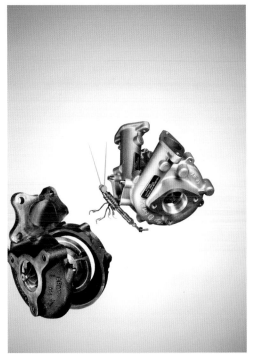

04

05

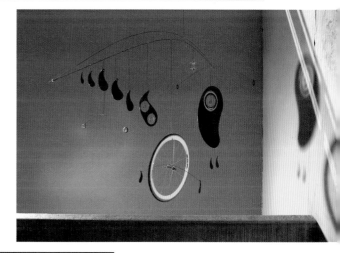

WHAT ARE THE BEST AND WORST EXPERIENCES BY FAR?

The best experience was when we created the campaign for Nissan in Amsterdam. It was so organised and it's the perfect job for us. We were so focused on the work, thanks to the producer.

We often do everything by ourselves for our own projects, and it's quite tricky because each of us tends to do more than we need, like the Rinascente windows, our first big project created in the south of Italy.

ARE YOU THREE VERY DIFFERENT INDIVIDUALS?

Yes, for sure we are three unique individuals, that's why we struggle often but this keeps us conscious of everyone's skills and opinions.

HOW DO YOU THREE WORK TOGETHER? WHAT WOULD YOU DO IF YOU ARE STANDING AT THREE EXTREMES AND FAIL TO REACH A CONSENSUS?

We work in stages, and everyone has a different job to do. If we ever fail to reach a consensus, at least the one who wins the debate is less hurt.

DO YOU INTEND TO RETAIN YOUR PRACTICE'S CURRENT SIZE? IF IT HAS TO GROW BIG ONE DAY, WHAT WOULD BE THE ULTIMATE SIZE?

Yes, for now we retain our current company size, unless 2013 reserves us maybe some good news and prospects of work.

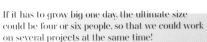

If it has to grow big one day, the ultimate size could be four or six people, so that we could work on several projects at the same time!

AND THE TRADITION(S)/ETHOS TO KEEP?

A funny and alive workplace with a lot a music and friends.

06

01 / Damaged for WAD Issue #52_2012
Art direction and set design on the theme of cosmetics. Photos by Fabrice Fouillet, and retouched by Franck Miatello. Special credits: Camille Hernandez.

02 / Stella by Stella_2010
A monumental rose handmade for Stella McCartney's new perfume. Photos by Caroline Fayette, Daniel Meyer. Sponsored by Arjowiggins Creative Papers.

03 / Cinqfruits_2011
Experimental installation and photography for Le Creative Sweatshop's blog, Cinqfruits.

04 / Nissan Parts_2012
Animal figures promoting remanufactured parts. Photos by Fabrice Fouillet.

05 / Destructured for WAD_2011
Sculptures on the theme of urban travelling. Photos by Ben Sandler and retouched by Pierrick le Gros. Bike component supplied by As De Pique. Special credits: Julien Drapier, Alex Sossah, Ditte.

06 / Africa Ban Data_2011
Infographics exploring paper fabrication using bamboo. Photos by Davina Muller. Sponsored by Arjowiggins Creative Papers.

07 / Talk_2010
Set seeing luxury as a craftwork with unusual materials. Photos by Davina Muller, retouched by Delphine Deguilhem. Make-up by Yann Boussand Larcher II. Hair by Sandra Lamzabi Yazoue. Model: Moon Kyu Lee..

07

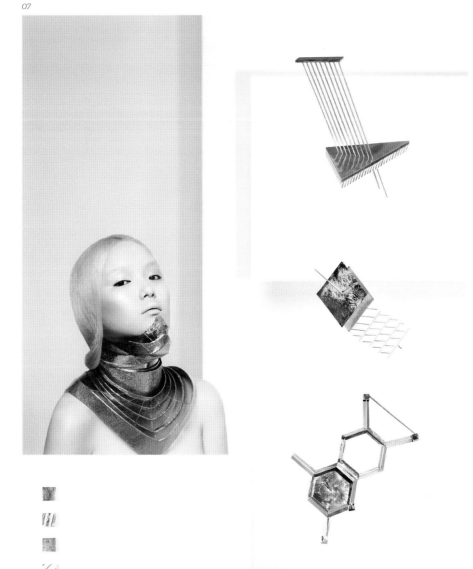

"We are serious
about humour."

Noted for its industrial approach to graphic design,
Lo Siento was set up by Spanish-born Borja Martinez
in 2006 at London College of Communication,
in search of an alliance with the artisan processes.
Amongst their celebrated packaging designs,
music covers and graphic identity projects composed
for restaurants and film production firms, the
Barcelona-based agency have also recently initiated
a range of typographical explorations, featuring
architectural lettering and bubble wrap typography
for magazines and campaigns.

LO SIENTO
Barcelona, Spain

Key members / Borja Martinez,
Gerard Miró, Cristina Vila i Nadal
Specialty / Graphic design
URL / www.losiento.net

Est. 2006

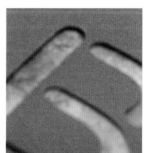

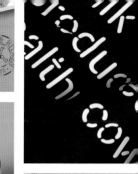

HOW DID YOU START YOUR COMPANY? WHAT IS/ARE YOUR CREED(S) AND ASPIRATION(S)?

In 2006, Borja Martínez founded Lo Siento on his own, where he started developing different graphic design and art direction projects for clients such as Sandro Desii, The Pinker Tones, Txoco, Roca, El Bulli, Macaco and Easyled, and awarded the Grand Laus by the FAD (Fomento de las Artes Decorativas) in 2010.

Nowadays the studio is specially interested in identity projects as a whole, with a physical and material approach to graphic solutions, resulting in a field where graphic and industrial go hand in hand, in a constant search for an alliance with the artisan processes.

Continue as we are working today, with the same intensity and passion, we bring in the best in every project because one's best creativity arises when you're having fun. We are serious about humour while elaborating handmade pieces with today's tools.

WHAT HAS BEEN DIFFICULT FOR YOU AT THE BEGINNING?

Finding creative freedom and the medium to optimise the project's finish. Funding is also an important issue in order to afford the purchase of essential tools in our work. On the other hand, it is tough to economically evaluate what you do with things that are always difficult to control. That also included many aspects of administration work and management issues of the office.

WHAT ROLES DO YOU INDIVIDUALLY PLAY IN THE FIRM?

I am the creative director and graphic designer, Gerard Miró is the paper engineer and production manager; Cristina Vila i Nadal is an important junior graphic designer.

HOW DO YOU PROMOTE YOURSELF?

Word of mouth, and nowadays our website and Facebook are the main devices of promotion at Lo Siento. But the crucial one, at the beginning and now, is word of mouth. I always thought that if you create a successful design, this will work for itself as an agent and promote your way of working and, therefore, your name as a graphic agency.

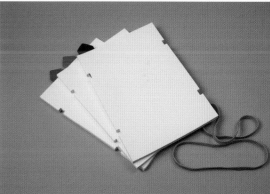

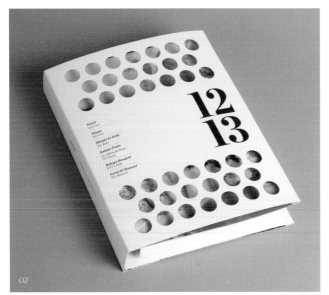

02

Make attempts, and focus on the type of work we do.

Being small allows us to tackle projects with a more intimate point as we are close to our customers which allows the process to be more comfortable. The structure also allows us to take up many small projects — that is what makes the graphic design studio sustainable. A large structure allows you to do fewer but larger projects.

IT MIGHT BE EASIER FOR LARGE DESIGN AGENCIES TO WIN A JOB. WHAT ARE YOUR STRATEGIES TO BEAT THEM? HAVE YOU EVER LOST HAD TO GIVE UP AN OPPORTUNITY THAT MIGHT BE RELEVANT TO YOUR COMPANY SIZE?

A situation like this does not often happen to us. but when this happens, we'll assume the risks. We try to participate in paid pitch to keep the impact on our little structure to a lesser extent. Winning is always difficult, but it'll make us more accessible to the commissioner or client. We also have lower rates, lower than big agencies, which will be an extra advantage to the client if our creative solution is on the same level as what big agencies provide.

WHAT ARE THE BEST AND WORST EXPERIENCES BY FAR?

The worst experience has been losing a client before I can provide a solution; the best thing is to work with genuine people who value how we work.

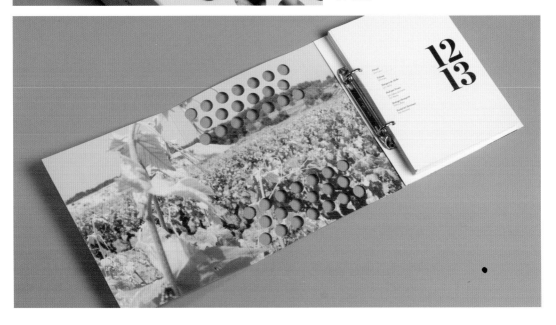

Soluciones
arquitectónicas
a medida

METRIC

RAFAEL GIL
Ca Alegre de Dalt nº 55-57
Primero, puerta A
Barcelona 08024
T 933 072 398
M 687 606 865
r.gil@metricbcn.com
www.metricbcn.com

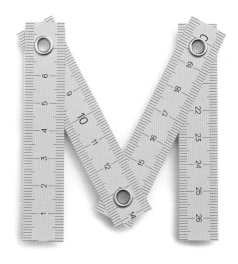

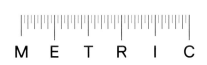

M E T R I C

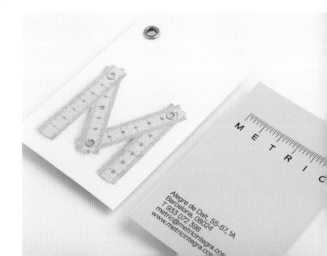

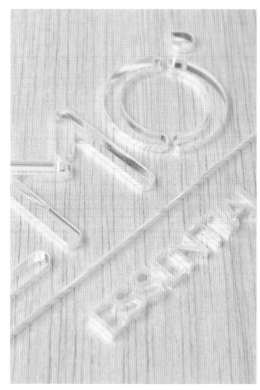

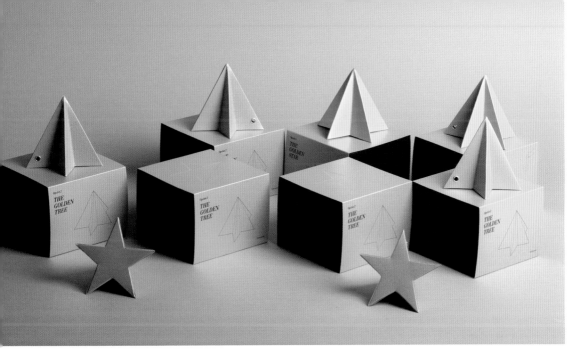

05

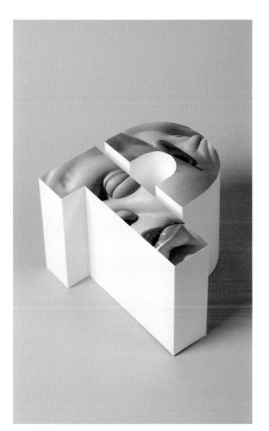

ARE YOU THREE VERY DIFFERENT INDIVIDUALS?

Not really. We all have the same main goals, similar taste for food, music or culture.

HOW DO YOU THREE WORK TOGETHER? WHAT WOULD YOU DO IF YOU ARE STANDING AT THREE EXTREMES AND FAIL TO REACH A CONSENSUS?

I lead the design process as a creative director. Cristina does the graphic system and applications and Gerard executes all three-dimensional paper structures or 3D typography. Each of us works independently and know how to take the right and appropriate decisions.

IF YOUR STUDIO HAS TO GROW BIG ONE DAY, WHAT WOULD BE THE ULTIMATE SIZE AND THE TRADITION(S) ETHOS TO KEEP?

I agree with Tibor Kalman that the most difficult thing about running a design company is not to grow, but growing keeps you away from the design process and convert your role of a designer into a director or organiser.

A maximum of 10 people. I will try to continue with the same system, passion and attitude towards humour as we do today but in gradually better ways.

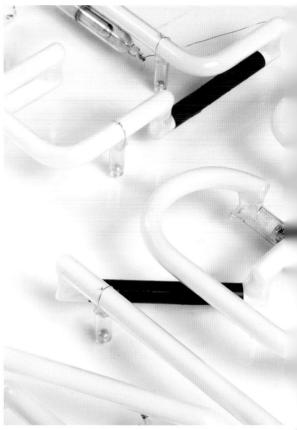

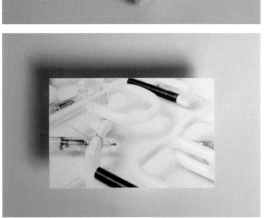

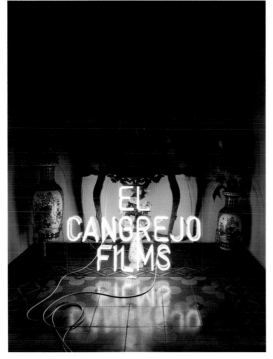

EVA BERGMAN
Production

Paseo de la Barceloneta 32, IA
Barcelona 08024
P+34 934 238 556
F+34 934 238 556
eva@fruitsandfilms.com
www.fruitsandfilms.com

EVA BERGMAN
Production

Paseo de la Barceloneta 32, IA
Barcelona 08024
P+34 934 238 556
F+34 934 238 556
eva@fruitsandfilms.com
www.fruitsandfilms.com

09

08

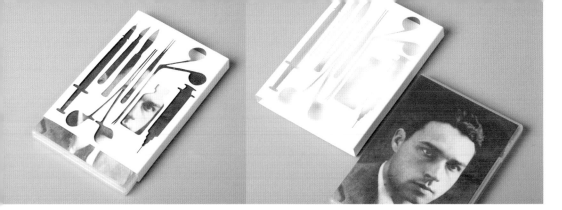

12

01 / BLANCA_2013
Visual identity for a dairy hub in the Pyrenees. Photos by Javier Tles.

02 / Parxet 2012/13 Catalogue_2012
Winery catalogue design.

03 / Metric Integra_2011
Identity for an architectural design and construction studio in Barcelona.

04 / Essential EMO_2011
Special wood packaging for an energy harmoniser product.

05 / XMAS GIFT_2012
A paper golden star-shape packaging that doubles as a tree.

06, 13 / The Private Space Opening_2011
Opening invite and identity for a multi-functional gallery space in Barcelona.

07 / Principal Art_2011
Identity for an art gallery in Barcelona.

08 / EL CANGREJO films_2009
Art direction and identity for an advertising and TV production company.

09 / Fruits&Films_2013
Identity for a production house in Barcelona.

10 / Moisés Broggy Documentary_2011
DVD case packaging proposal for Dr. Broggy's documentary.

11 / Zuka_2011
Japanese restaurant identity. Photos by Diaz Wichmann.

12 / Vila Florida_2011
Packaging and identity for a bar and restaurant set inside a civic center with garden.

13

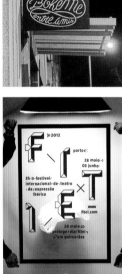

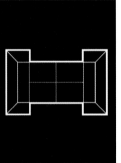

"If we do our job well, the choice is not about big or small, but between good and badly done."

THIS IS PACIFICA
Porto, Portugal

Key members / Pedro Serrão, Pedro Mesquita, Filipe Mesquita
Specialties / Branding, Graphic design
URL / www.thisispacifica.com

Est. 2007

This Is Pacifica is an independent design studio based in Porto, Portugal, established by Pedro Serrão, Pedro Mesquita and Filipe Mesquita in 2007. Laying stress on forward-thinking and creative approaches, the team promises to bring a wealth of knowledge and enthusiasm to every new project ranging from motion graphics to exhibitions and web design. Pacifica believes in creating ideas, solutions and opportunities based on visual thinking and creative approach.

01

HOW DID YOU START YOUR COMPANY? WHAT IS /ARE YOUR CREED(S) AND ASPIRATION(S)?

Pacifica was born in 2007. The studio combines the vision and ambition of its three founders to overcome all necessary challenges and put their best on every work, however small or large it is. We add layers of meaning to the work with solid concepts in order to make it assertive, and not just yielding to the temptation to solve each work only with aesthetic assumptions.

WHAT HAS BEEN DIFFICULT FOR YOU AT THE BEGINNING?

In the beginning, the difficult part has been to find a space that suited our identity and allowed us to make more manual and crafted work. And, of course, the client managing part, together with budget and timing. That requires some experience.

WHAT ROLES DO YOU INDIVIDUALLY PLAY IN THE FIRM?

Each of us plays the role of a creative director on a series of projects and subsequently interferes in projects for which each is responsible. We're not interested in leaving marks of individual style. We believe that the projects' values derive from an approach adjusted to the project's refined conceptual universe. We are interested in genuine understanding and the delivery of opinions and vision. We are not looking for style, but good ideas.

HOW DO YOU PROMOTE YOURSELF?

Our name are mainly publicised as we're recognised by awards, or appear in magazine articles or participate in books. Another way that has given us some visibility is our presence in juries at international design and advertising competitions, such as the Cannes Lions Awards, the Art Directors Club of Europe Awards or the El Ojo de Iberoamérica Awards.

Recently we have also launched a visual manifesto that reveals our conceptual approach to our different projects, called Forward Thinking — The essential instances by This is Pacifica. The video series can be viewed on our website and on vimeo.

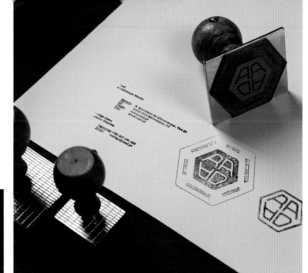

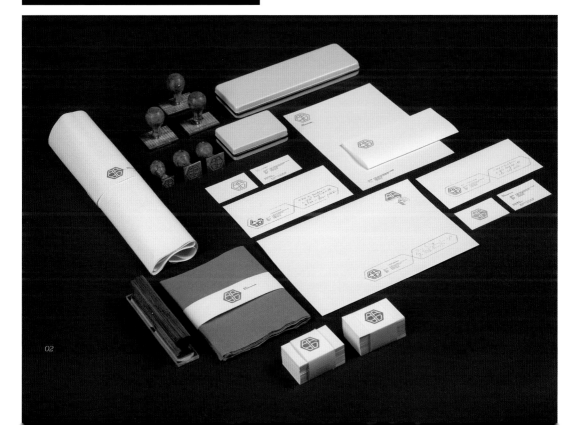

03

04

WHAT MAKE(S) SMALL STUDIOS SUSTAINABLE? WHAT IS MOST CRITICAL FOR STUDIOS LIKE YOURS TO GAIN A FOOTHOLD IN THE COMPETITIVE MARKET?

In Pacifica, we say to customers that we are a studio for special projects, projects that require a more client-side intimate involvement with the design studio, that can originate moments of inspiration. This approach is only possible when a studio can fully embrace a design. We also believe that brands, clients and consumers increasingly identify with this kind of cooperation and philosophy. Small is the new big.

IT MIGHT BE EASIER FOR LARGE DESIGN AGENCIES TO WIN A JOB. WHAT ARE YOUR STRATEGIES TO BEAT THEM? HAVE YOU EVER LOST HAD TO GIVE UP AN OPPORTUNITY THAT MIGHT BE RELEVANT TO YOUR COMPANY SIZE?

Job well done. If we do our job well, the choice is not about big or small, but between good and badly done. If we do our job well, if the concept is consistent and fresh, execution and materialisation blameless, the studio scale is nullified and the responsibility of choice increased. It is obvious that the choice is not always between good or bad. There are other issues that lead to the decision to something tangible and more subjective. Most recently we have worked in partnership with international and Portuguese advertising agencies for large customers like Coca-Cola on special projects where our participation and expertise are valuable.

WHAT ARE THE BEST AND WORST EXPERIENCES BY FAR?

The best experiences are varied: customer satisfaction, the success of campaigns or images we created, the awards we have won, the recognition not only by the public but also professionals in our fields, like RAAD, La Bohème, FITEI, OFFE, AVA and Red Bull Music Academy, etc.. The worst is when our work is not interrupted by the client's will but by external issues like the lack of budgets or economic conjecture.

ARE YOU THREE VERY DIFFERENT INDIVIDUALS?

We are all different, although two of the three are twin brothers. The three are very different in terms of personality, temperament and the way we work, but that unites us with great respect for difference and pride in the union.

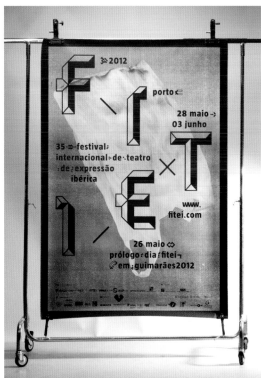

05

HOW DO YOU THREE WORK TOGETHER? WHAT WOULD YOU DO IF YOU ARE STANDING AT THREE EXTREMES AND FAIL TO REACH A CONSENSUS?

We work with an open mind. We are curious and passionate about what we do and ambitious in what we can achieve. We specially love telling good stories and sharing our vision. When this is so, at the end of the day, things make sense, because the work is a result of a sum of different layers that add together tell a story of complexity.

DO YOU INTEND TO RETAIN YOUR PRACTICE'S CURRENT SIZE? IF IT HAS TO GROW BIG ONE DAY, WHAT WOULD BE THE ULTIMATE SIZE AND THE TRADITION(S) ETHOS TO KEEP?

We've thought about it. We believe in working increasingly with new markets such as the ones in Europe (we are developing projects in Germany, England and Spain), the Portuguese-speaking countries, such as Brazil (with whom we want to establish more contacts and projects) and Angola (where we are currently establishing partner) and even emerging markets (we are about to close a project in Lebanon). We don't know yet if we will have to grow to meet all demands. We prefer to choose the best projects than to grow a lot. But there is margin to growth while keeping the quality that we want in our work.

Growing or not, we want to keep us faithful to all principles that motivated us to open our own studio. If we loose this we abdicate our identity. We are Portuguese based in Portugal but we work for the world. Too often we have interns from around the world coming to learn and share knowledge. We want to work with and for people whoever wants to work with us.

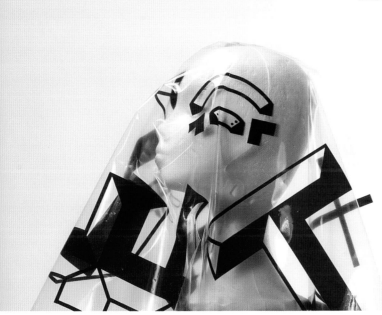

06

07

01 / FITEI 34_2011
Collateral for the 34th International
Theatre Festival of Iberian Expressions
(FITEI).

02 / RAAD_2012
Identity for an architeture and interior
design studio in Porto. Photos by Softbox.

03 / Red Bull Music Academy_2011
Communications for the music academy's event held in Porto.

04 / FITEI 33_2010
Collateral that explores a scene of distress
and surprise for the 33th FITEI.

05 / FITEI 35_2012
Identity for the 35th FITEI that assumes
an attitude of social responsibility.

06 / Zilian_2012
Opening invite for a new store in Braga.

07 / Rua Aberta_2012
Photo-based communications for an
"open street" event.

3R
IO

SO1O · 2UO · 3RIO
Small Studio · Great Impact

First published and distributed by
viction:workshop ltd.

viction:ary™

viction:workshop ltd.
Unit C, 7/F, Seabright Plaza, 9-23 Shell Street,
North Point, Hong Kong
Url: www.victionary.com   Email: we@victionary.com
www.facebook.com/victionworkshop
www.twitter.com/victionary_
www.weibo.com/victionary

Edited and produced by viction:ary

Concepts & art direction by Victor Cheung
Book design by viction:workshop ltd.
Cover image on slipcase by Designbolaget

ISBN 978-988-19439-1-0

Printed and bound in China

Acknowledgements

We would like to thank all the designers and companies who have involved in
the production of this book. This project would not have been accomplished
without their significant contribution to the compilation of this book. We would
also like to express our gratitude to all the producers for their invaluable
opinions and assistance throughout this entire project. The successful
completion also owes a great deal to many professionals in the creative
industry who have given us precious insights and comments. And to the many
others whose names are not credited but have made specific input in this
book, we thank you for your continuous support the whole time.

Future Editions

If you wish to participate in viction:ary's future projects and publications,
please send your website or portfolio to submit@victionary.com